D0837959

Centerpointe Research Institute
1600 NW 167th Place, Suite 320
Beaverton, OR 97006

Telephone Hotline (503) 672-7117
Order Line (800) 945-2741
Fax number (503) 643-3114
email support: support@centerpointe.com
web page: www.centerpointe.com

Managing
Evolutionary Growth

*How to Create Deep Change
Without Falling Apart*

BY

BILL HARRIS

COMPILED FOR PARTICIPANTS OF THE HOLOSYNC SOLUTION™ PROGRAM

CENTERPOINTE RESEARCH INSTITUTE

CONTENTS

Acknowledgements

We would like to thank transpersonal psychotherapist Dr. Beverlee Marks Taub, Ph.D. for her input on the sections of this manual dealing with the integration of emotional and mental catharsis, and holistic health guide Ron Mink for his input on the sections dealing with physical catharsis. In addition, we are indebted to Michael Hutchison for his discussion of the work of Ilya Prigogine in his book, MegaBrain.

Preface

Possibly the greatest skill one can acquire as a participant in The Holosync Solution™ is the ability to identify, take responsibility for, and move through the upheaval which sometimes accompanies deep meditation. We call this evolutionary catharsis because without it there is no growth, no expansion of awareness, no evolution. Catharsis is, in fact, the proof that evolution is happening, that the process is working.

The guidelines in this booklet are the result of many years of research and many thousands of hours of meditation practice. They will allow you to move through your experience with minimum discomfort and maximum growth. The end result is a powerful experience of your own perfection; an experience of connectedness, peace, and happiness; a life experience cleansed of fears, dysfunctional and self-destructive behaviors, conflict, and debilitating emotional pain. Along the way, you will meet all the aspects of yourself and of your world that you knowingly or unknowingly have deemed to be inappropriate and have tried to repress. Some of this you will not want to look at; some you will move through easily. Your experience, whatever it may be, is the result of what lies inside you and will be unique to you.

The material in this booklet will mean more to you after you have some experience with the program. Some things you may not experience for several years, some could happen immediately, some of it never. Since what you read will very likely have no impact until you actually have the experience under discussion, it would be wise to re-read this material every so often and use this booklet as a reference manual when you feel stuck.

That this booklet emphasizes the more difficult and unpleasant aspects of personal growth should not lead you to believe that this will be your your predominant experience. This program is a great adventure filled with peace, happiness, joy, and aliveness. To begin this process fearing the painful aspects of evolutionary growth would be like reading about every manner of injury sustainable in an automobile crash and then, thinking that serious injury is the essence of driving, approaching it with fear. Our purpose is not to scare you but rather to ensure that you will have all the information you need to deal successfully with whatever happens.

Positive core-level change at the accelerated pace brought about by The Holosync Solution can be cathartic. It is also a fascinating journey where each breakthrough is more amazing and fulfilling than the last. Catharsis need not be painful—you are the creator of your experience, and much of this program is about learning how to create growth without suffering.

What is Catharsis?

Webster defines catharsis as "a purifying release of the emotions or of tension by bringing repressed material to consciousness." This is a natural result of the intensified meditation practice of those who use The Holosync Solution soundtracks. Catharsis involves the upheaval, intensification and release of familiar or habitual mental, emotional and physical patterns operating from the unconscious parts of the mind. The end result is a new way of seeing and experiencing "what is," and a reorganization of the brain at a new and more evolved level—one that allows a greater perception and experience of the infinite number of connections making up our true nature as the one energy of all and everything.

The suppression and relegation of certain mental and emotional material to the unconscious is a natural result of dualistic thinking, of dividing the universe into that which is "appropriate" and that which is "inappropriate." Because our mental and emotional *resistance* to that which we term inappropriate causes pain, much energy is expended in keeping this material out of conscious awareness. Only by coming to terms with this self-created "dark side" do we grow and evolve. By seeing this material as one side of a polarity, we create separation and blind ourselves to the perfection and connectedness that is actually

1

there. Reaching the point where every manifestation, whether in ourself or in our world, is seen as neither appropriate nor inappropriate but as simply "happening," then and only then can we experience our lives as the peaceful, radiantly healthy, mentally and spiritually fulfilling adventure it was meant to be.

In understanding evolutionary change and the cathartic upheaval that accompanies it, we will first need to explore how the brain evolves, and why. As evolution happens, the brain is irrevocably altered—patterns of electrical energy moving through the brain are changed, individual neurons in the cerebral cortex change the number and shape of their dendrites and synapses, and new patterns linking neurons to each other are created. All of this results in new networks of message transmission and, ultimately, new states of mind and new ways of seeing and experiencing, allowing us not only to understand intellectually but to actually experience ourselves as the connectedness, the flux, the flow of all and everything. But what causes these changes? Why does the brain evolve, continually reorganizing itself at higher and more functional levels? And what does this have to do with evolutionary growth and catharsis?

Order Out of Chaos:

Ilya Prigogine and the second law of thermodynamics

The answer to this question is found in the Nobel Prize-winning work of the Russian-born Belgian theoretical chemist, Ilya Prigogine. Prigogine, working in the field of thermodynamics (the branch of physics that deals with the relationship between heat and work), became intensely curious about what seemed to be a major contradiction between one of the basic laws of science and some equally basic observable facts, including the existence and evolution of life itself.

The second law of thermodynamics states that whenever work is done, some energy is irretrievably lost. When expanding steam causes a piston to move, for instance, some energy is lost from the system in the form of heat radiation due to friction. In addition, the machine itself, over time (unless energy is added to the system in the form of an overhaul, new parts, etc.) will wear out and eventually break down.

All machines, in fact, must eventually break down, and scientists have confirmed that the law describing this energy exchange in a machine applies to all energy systems in the universe. This fact of nature is often spoken of as the law of increasing entropy. Entropy, simply put, is a measure of the amount of randomness or chaos in a system, and the law of increasing entropy is an expression of the fact the the universe is ir-

3

reversibly moving toward a state of increased disorder and randomness. Left to itself, with no energy input from the outside, any system will tend to break down and become increasingly disordered. A car will turn to rust and fall apart, a mountain will eventually be worn down, and so on. Even the expansion of the universe itself is a movement in the direction of increasing disorder, increasing entropy.

Yet we can plainly see that many things in the universe tend toward *increased* order—the opposite of what is predicted by the second law of thermodynamics. Life itself has evolved as atoms became molecules, then amino acids, proteins, cells, multi-cellular life, social systems, and so on—definitely a process of increasing order, and obviously against the flow of increasing entropy. How can this be? This seeming paradox puzzled scientists for over a hundred years until Prigogine discovered the key: **that order arises not in spite of entropy, but because of it!**

Dissipative Structures

The scientific community had, to this point, been more interested in studying idealized closed systems, systems that have no interaction with the surrounding environment —the activity of a certain number of molecules of hydrogen in a closed container, for instance, or an ideal machine. In the real world, of course, there is really no such thing as a closed system (a pile of sand, a brick, a piece of plastic, or the furniture in your living room are for all intents and purposes closed systems because their interactions with their environment happen so slowly as to have little effect, but they, too, are open systems when a longer time frame is considered).

Closed systems soon reach an equilibrium state of maximum disorder—the molecules of hydrogen in the closed container spread out and their tendency to accidently become more ordered is immediately cancelled out by an offsetting tendency toward increasing disorder, so that the net effect is one of maintaining an equilibrium state of maximum entropy.

Prigogine, on the other hand, was interested in open systems, those that constantly interact with their environment, changing, growing, and evolving. Living things are prime examples of open systems. Far from equilibrium, they constantly take in energy in the form of light, heat, nutrients, air, water, etc., and at the same time dissipate

5

to their environment carbon dioxide, heat, waste products, various activities, and so on. In this way they are constantly adjusting to their environment, changing, growing, healing, learning.

Prigogine set out to study these open systems in an effort to solve the riddle of why and how systems of increasing order can exist in a universe inevitably tending toward disorder and chaos. Studying certain far-from-equilibrium chemical processes—open systems which, when heated, exhibited increased order and growth—he obtained results which again seemed to contradict the second law of thermodynamics. That is, until he ascertained that while the system itself did indeed become increasingly ordered, it did so by dispersing entropy to its environment! These experiments and Prigogine's mathematical analysis of them proved his hypothesis that order emerges not in spite of chaos but *because* of it—that evolution and growth are the inevitable product of far-from-equilibrium (open) systems. The key to such systems is their ability not only to take in energy and matter from the environment, but also to dissipate the resulting entropy to the environment, creating an overall energy dynamic that *does* follow the second law of thermodynamics.

Progigine called these open systems that evolve and grow by taking in energy and matter from their environment and then dissipating the resulting entropy into their environment *dissipative structures*. Scientists have since confirmed that Prigogine's discoveries regarding dissipative structures apply to every open system in the universe, whether a chemical system (as in Prigogine's original experiments), a seed, a highway system, a corporation, or a human being. Such structures, in order to maintain their existence, must interact with their environment, continually maintaining the flow of energy into and out of the system. And, rather than being the structure through which energy and matter flow, dissipative structures are, in fact, the flow itelf. This supports a view, reached independently by quantum mechanical physicists, that the universe is not one of independent *things*, but rather one of *process*, a changing, flowing, evolving, and intimately interconnected system of interactions.

Evolutionary Growth:

"Escape into a higher order"

Dissipative structures flourish in unstable, fluctuating environments by being plastic enough to handle the variations and changes in such environments. The more ordered and complex a system becomes, the more entropy it must dissipate in order to maintain its existence. Conversely, each system has an upper limit, due to its level of complexity, of how much entropy it can dissipate. *This is a key point.* If the fluctuations from the environment increase beyond that limit, the system, unable to disperse enough entropy into its environment, begins to become internally more entropic, or chaotic.

If the excessive fluctuations continue, the chaos eventually becomes so great that the system begins to break down until finally a point is reached where the slightest nudge can bring the whole system grinding to a halt. This point, which Prigogine called a *bifurcation point*—bifurcate means to divide into two branches—is a decision point, a moment of truth. Either the system totally breaks down and ceases to exist as an organized system or it spontaneously reorders itself in an entirely new way. Incredibly, this reorganization is non-causal and non-linear with what went before—it is in no way predictable from prior conditions. Only the probability of a certain outcome can be determined. The change is a true quantum leap, a death and rebirth, and the main characteristic of the new system is that *it has the capability to handle the fluctuations, the input from the environment, that caused the initial overwhelm and eventual breakdown of the old system.* In Prigogine's words, the system "escapes into a higher order." Out of chaos comes a new order, a more evolved system. This new system has a new stability and is able to more easily exist in the previously overwhelming high fluctuation environment. But if fluctuations increase again to a level beyond the system's new and higher capacity for dispersion of entropy, the process will repeat, resulting in new internal chaos and another reorganization at a new and yet more evolved level.

The Human Brain as a Dissipative Structure

❦

The human brain is the ultimate dissipative structure, constantly taking in energy and matter from the environment, constantly dispersing entropy. We are able to handle amazing amounts of fluctuation from the environment, encountering all kinds of new ideas, stimuli, and events, handling them without threat to the system. But if fluctuations reach a certain critical point, different for each individual, we begin to feel overwhelmed and become less and less able to deal with increased environmental input. Eventually, the system (our mental construct of "what is") is forced either to break down or to reorganize at a higher, more evolved level. The process goes something like this: first things make sense; then, as chaos increases, they no longer make sense any more; finally, after reorganization, they make sense again, but in a *whole new way, never before imagined.*

It is easy to see from the foregoing discussion that certain types of people will be more likely to reach this "moment of truth"—what Abraham Maslow called "peak experience"—and give themselves the chance of "escaping into a higher order." Those who constantly open themselves to new ideas and experiences and who are not afraid of feeling a bit overwhelmed once in a while are more likely to have this type of peak experience and are therefore more likely to evolve. On the other hand, people who resist any new idea, who hate to try new experiences, who reject anything that does not fit the structure of their belief system and never experience any doubts about their way of seeing things—in other words, people who resist the influx of new energy, stumuli, ideas, and matter into their brains—almost never have peak experiences and evolve very slowly, if at all.

If the fluctuations affecting the brain are strong enough, however, even a brain strongly resistant to change can be impacted. This, indeed is what happens when we meditate using Holosync. Holosync technology creates fluctuations in the brain that eventually affect even our deepest, most subconscious layers of resistance, bringing about change at a very deep and profound level—forcing the brain to reorganize at more and more evolved levels. Eventually the brain evolves to a point where it is able to perceive, experience, and be one with the interconnections of the entire universe, allowing the release and healing of addictive and dysfunctional patterns and the growth of an internal sense of peace with oneself and with one's world.

High-Fluctuation Brain Wave States and Evolution

What is it, then, about the alpha, theta, and delta brain wave states that affects the brain in this way? High frequency brain wave states, such as the beta state, have very low amplitude. Low amplitude means the wave form has little difference from its highest to its lowest point—in other words, only a small amount of fluctuation. Low frequency brain waves, however, such as those in the delta range, have very high amplitude—a large amount of fluctuation. When in the beta state, characteristic of external attention and ordinary waking consciousness, the brain experiences little fluctuation. Since the amount of environmental fluctuation experienced by a dissipative structure determines its possibilities for quantum evolutionary change, the brain when in a beta state is not pushed to grow and evolve. In the alpha, theta, and delta states, however, the brain experiences larger fluctuations, which, as we have seen, stimulates evolutionary change in dissipative structures.

Michael Hutchison, in his book *MegaBrain*, gives the example of a large group of people crossing a bridge. If each walks at his own rhythm, the resulting sound of the footsteps will be high frequency (someone's foot will hit the bridge each fraction of a second) and the fluctuations of the bridge itself will be of low (in fact, imperceptible) amplitude. However, if everyone walks in step to the same rhythm, the frequency of the footsteps will be much lower (perhaps two steps each second) and the fluctuations of a much higher amplitude. If there are enough people walking in step with one another, the fluctuations can become so great that the bridge cannot dissipate the entropy. Since the bridge is essentially a closed system and cannot evolve to a higher order, it collapses. On the other hand, when an open system like the human brain is exposed to such low-frequency, high- amplitude fluctuations, it can (and will) make the quantum leap to the next higher level of organization.

In addition to the effect on the brain of daily exposure to the alpha, theta, and delta brain wave states, we are also, as we move through each succeedingly deeper level of the program, inducing the alpha, theta, and delta brain wave states with increasingly lower, more high-amplitude frequencies. We are also giving the brain much new input through the use of life-affirming, self-empowering subliminal affirmations. All of this causes enormous fluctuations in the brain, bringing one frequently to peak experience and causing a great acceleration in the evolutionary growth process, continually pushing the brain to evolve by "escaping into a higher order."

This whole process of dissipative strutures evolving into more complex states in order to handle increased energy flow explains several of the observed reactions of participants in The Holosync Solution. One is that as people move through the various levels of the program they find that people and events to which they once reacted with stress and discomfort no longer seem to bother them, that they are somehow able to "go with the flow" of what is happening more easily. This is exactly how we would expect a dissipative structure, having reorganized itself at a higher level, to behave. Fluctuations that once put stress on the system are now easily handled. This is because the more evolved system, as a way of maintaining its structure, has developed the ability to dissipate the increased entropy into its environment, something it previously could not do.

The second behavior we observe in some program participants is an occasional and temporary increase in self-defeating and dysfuntional behaviors as participants come to the point of peak experience in daily use of Holosync soundtracks. These behaviors, learned in childhood as survival methods in particular family situations, fall into three categories: 1) those that try to reduce the amount of overwhelm by desperately trying to push entropy out of the system, 2) those that seek to block additional energy from entering the system, and 3) those that seek to distract one from feeling the growing internal chaos as the system approaches the evolutionary "moment of truth."

Behaviors that seek to frantically *disperse* entropy can include anything of a dissipative nature—yelling, screaming, crying, talking, running, jumping, compulsive behaviors, sexual activity, physical ailments—anything that dissipates energy. Behaviors that attempt to *block* additional incoming energy include depression, withdrawal, loss of appetite, and sickness. Behaviors that distract one from the feeling of overwhelm could include alchohol and drug use, sexual activity, food addiction, dissociation, watching television, reading—anything that either distracts or deadens one to the flow of energy. It is worth noting that attempts to block incoming energy rarely succeed and over time often result in attempts by the body to dissipate the entropy physically, often in the form of debilitating or life-threatening diseases.

We see, then, that *dysfunctional behaviors, including all varieties of addictions (not only to alcohol and drugs but also to sex, food, relationships, indebtedness, etc.) are means, albeit self-destructive ones, of dealing with overwhelming input from the environment.* As the fluctuations to the brain bring us to the point of peak experience—in other words, as the "moment of truth," where the system either breaks down or evolves to a higher order, approaches—we pull out all the stops in a desperate, last-ditch effort (ironically) to preserve the current system. Our goal, however, is not to dissipate this energy or to block it from entering the system, but to be with it and experience it in such a way that the system can easily and naturally reorganize itself at a more evolved level. Once this happens, the previously overwhelming environmental fluctuations are easily handled and the necessary entropy is dissipated naturally without the need for these desperate and dysfunctional behaviors.

It is important to remember that we are not the system, but rather *the evolutionary process itself.* The system is nothing but our ego, and the ego is but a conceptualization of ourself and our relationship to our world. To evolve is to be constantly updating this conceptualization until it ultimately includes all of the interrelationships that make up who we really are, our interconnectedness with the entire universe. Desperate attempts to save an overwhelmed system only inhibit the evolutionary process and are based on the illusion that we are our ego, that we are a concept of ourself rather than the thing itself. While the ego is a useful (though limited) Map of Reality, confusing the map for the actual territory is one of the most limiting things a human being can do.

In moving through The Holosync Solution—or for that matter, any type of personal growth process—it is crucial that one begin to notice which behaviors, in moments of temporary overwhelm, are attempts to block or deaden the incoming energy and which are attempts to frantically dissipate entropy into the environment. While these behaviors may help to release the pressure temporarily, the end result is that of keeping the system the way that it is. Since we want the system to have every opportunity to make the quantum leap to the next higher level of awareness, these blocking and dissipating behaviors are to be minimized. Learning to sit quietly and be with whatever is happening, without trying to desperately push the energy out, or learning to get the energy flowing again if we have been unconsciously trying to block it from flowing in, will allow reorganization at a more evolved level to happen smoothly and easily. And, ironically, indulging in these habitual non-evolutionary behaviors only makes the process more painful, which is what we were trying to avoid when we initiated these behaviors in the first place.

The ability to work with your upheaval in this manner does not develop all at once, however. These behaviors are automatic, unconscious, and very compelling. Particularly at first, the last thing you will feel like doing is giving up what seems to be a natural response to feeling overwhelmed.

In each deeper level of The Holosync Solution, we see participants from time to time falling back on the same repetoire of dysfunctional and self-defeating behaviors in an attempt to dissipate the increased entropy of a system coming to peak experience. Although these behaviors generally become less pronounced as one moves through the different levels of the program, they do continue to manifest until a system finally evolves that can dissipate the entropy so these fluctuations no longer present a problem. At that point these behaviors, no longer necessary, are extinguished forever.

Many personal growth approaches are unfortunately nothing more than well-intentioned attempts to teach "healthier" ways of dissipating energy. This may temporarily relieve the tension but it also short-circuits the evolutionary process by not allowing the system to come to a point of peak experience. Dealing with these peak experiences in a whole new way, where the energy is not artificially dissipated but instead channeled into evolutionary growth, requires the development of much awareness and a "witnessing" attitude, a natural development of deep meditative practice. All of the suggestions in this booklet are really nothing more than methods to help you (1) identify your particular unconscious strategies for dealing with overwhelming energy input and (2) replace them with new strategies that support rather than interrupt the evolutionary process. If you will apply yourself to doing this, not only will you greatly accelerate your personal evolution, but you will also experience less pain in the process. As will be discussed later in more detail, the process of death and rebirth of *who we think we are* is not inherently painful. It is rather the *resistance* to the process that causes whatever pain we may feel.

With the foregoing theoretical basis for understanding the process of evolutionary change, we will now examine the way these changes manifest in the life experience of participants in The Holosync Solution. Remember that the following is an overview of the many different ways that cathartic changes can manifest, rather than a picture of what any one person will experience, and that even those who manifest the maximum amount of upheaval while moving through the different levels of this program are experiencing discomfort only a small proportion of the time. By following the suggestions offered in this book, you will be able to move through whatever comes up for you with a minimum amount of discomfort and take full advantage of the acceleration in evolutionary growth possible through use of Holosync soundtracks.

Experiences During Meditation

The meditation experiences reported by those using Holosync are the same experiences reported by advanced meditators of all times, places, and cultures. They include visions of various types, including dream-like sequences, colors, lights, geometrical shapes; the experience of various odors; auditory experiences such as music, voices and other sounds; the sensation of being either very large or very small, or of movement when one is actually still; euphoria, blissfulness, ecstasy; restlessness, boredom, anxiety and other types of physical discomfort, including pains in different parts of the body; jerking and twitching of different parts of the body; time distortion, where time seems to either speed up or slow down; the feeling of electric currents or other sensations moving up the spine; tingling or numbness in hands, arms, legs, face or top of the head; pressure at the location of different energy centers in the body (called *chakras* in the East), especially between the eyebrows, at the top of the head, and in the heart area; spontaneous rocking or swaying and other types of flowing movements; so-called "out of body" experiences; loss of body awareness; expanded awareness, including the experience of being a point of awareness with no actual volume or dimensions, profound insights, clarity, and peace; extremes of mentation, including a busy mind, obsessive thoughts, intense emotions; suspended mentation; loss of consciousness; even various psychic phenomena such as remote viewing, clairvoyance, clair-audience, out of body experiences, ESP, knowledge of the future, etc.

There are various explanations for these phenomena, but basically they are all the response of the nervous system to the lower and more powerful frequencies embedded in The Holosync Solution soundtracks. Increased life force energy flowing through the nervous system creates various physical, mental, emotional, and even metaphysical responses as the nervous system becomes more refined. Various psychic and metaphysical phenomena begin to manifest because the brain, as it is reformatted to take into account more of the connectedness of the universe, perceives more relationships and is able to communicate and sense the universe at a more refined level of awareness.

You may experience many of these phenomena or you may experience very few of them; the nature of the experience during meditation is relatively unimportant. These phenomena are merely responses in the nervous system to the system coming to peak experience and reorganizing itself at higher levels of organization.

Again, the most important prescription we can give is to simply *watch*, to be the curious witness to what is going on. Becoming involved with what is experienced during meditation, either by desiring or fearing the continuation or repetition of a given experience is a trap that will impede your progress. Whatever happens, watch with curiosity and full awareness, but without attachment. Everything that happens, no matter how compelling or disturbing (or boring), is merely a projection of your mind. What we seek, ultimately, is to go beyond these experiences, beyond the mind. Whatever you may experience, in or out of meditation, watch it and let it go.

Nodding out momentarily or even falling asleep during meditation, especially when using the Immersion soundtracks, is common at the beginning of each level. This is the nervous system's response to the new lower frequency moving through the nadis (see page 24) and encountering resistance in the form of untruthful belief systems and physical impurities. As you move through and integrate each level of the program, this response will diminish and eventually disappear. A thorough physical cleansing (which can take as long as 2-4 years) and a very pure diet will help to eliminate this response. (**See Appendix I**).

Sleep Experience

The increased expansion of awareness brought about by meditating with Holosync will also affect your sleep experience. In the beginning of each level, especially for the first three or four levels of the program, it is common to experience a few weeks of heightened dreaming, where dreams are often weird and extremely vivid. Since dream content can be a clue to unconscious belief systems, many participants like to keep their journal at their bedside so as to note their dream experiences immediately upon awakening before they slip away.

Intensity of dreaming may gradually turn to a lack of dreaming or to short dreams experienced right before waking that are often difficult or impossible to recall. Lack of dreaming is an indication that much sleep time is being spent in the delta brain wave state (the state of deep, dreamless sleep). Also, due to your daily meditation practice, there will no longer be the need for so much mental and emotional processing during sleep. The ability to spend more sleep time in the delta state is facilitated by 1) sleeping on your back (see program instructions), which allows the brain to more easily synchronize, 2) the Floating soundtrack, which enhances the brain's ability to stay in the delta state during sleep, and 3) the brain's increased ability to spontaneously synchronize due to your use of Holosync.

You may feel on some nights that you are not falling asleep at all. This is a common experience with advanced meditators and is called *sleep witnessing or lucid sleep*. It means that awareness remains while the body and mind are asleep. In this state you may experience dream-like or visionary experiences much like those during your regular daytime meditations. Witnessing is, at first, an odd sensation (you will find that it will come and go), but you will become accustomed to it. Witnessing or not, you will find that you *are* getting plenty of rest during the night.

Another common (though not universal) experience is that of needing significantly less sleep (4 to 5 hours is common). This is another result of spending more sleep time in the delta state, where we get our deepest and most restful sleep. Participants often awaken after four or five hours feeling extremely alert, experiencing a kind of super-awareness. But instead of getting up, they often roll over and go back to sleep for two or three more hours. This is due to entrenched belief systems regarding the need for sleep (and, of course, because sleeping feels good!). You might want to experiment with getting up if you experience this "4 a.m. wake up" and find out for yourself whether or not you really need more sleep.

At times when you are processing particularly intense subconscious material, you may find yourself sleeping more deeply and feeling groggy upon awakening. This is due to increased production of various neurochemicals which mask the pain of heavy internal catharsis. Yoga postures, physical exercise and alternate nostril breathing (see **Appendix I**) will help to revitalize you in the morning. Eating a banana or other sweet fruit will help, also.

Occasionally participants experience difficulty at first in sleeping with the Floating soundtrack, either because they are not used to the sleeping position or not used to sleeping while wearing headphones. If wearing the headphones becomes unbearably uncomfortable, remove them for the remainder of the night but always begin your sleep period with them again the next night. Within a week or two you should no longer have a problem wearing them. If you are gently persistent with yourself for several weeks and still cannot tolerate the headphones you may use speakers, one on each side of the bed. Since the headphones are much more effective, give them a good try before going to the use of speakers. (Remember also to play the Floating soundtrack at the lowest possible volume.)

As for your sleeping position, begin each sleep period on your back. If you wake up and find you have rolled over, return to your back. At times you may feel like you just cannot bear to be on your back for another minute; in that case, allow yourself to roll over—this is not designed to be torture. If you are persistant in trying to sleep on your back, it will soon become easy. Nearly everyone who keeps trying reports that they eventually prefer sleeping on their back to sleeping on their side and some even report that they cannot fall asleep in any other position!

Sleeping on your back, which allows the brain to more easily synchronize during sleep, allows deeper access to the mind's data banks enhancing the subliminal reformatting process in the brain. Because more sleep time is spent in delta, it also results in less sleep. Again, be gentle with yourself—there is no need to torture yourself.

Physical Release

There are three broad areas of cathartic release: physical, emotional, and mental. Physical catharsis is, first of all, the body's attempt to dissipate entropy that cannot be released on the more subtle mental or emotional levels. In the initial stages of the program, however, physical catharsis is often nothing more than purification of the body—the release of toxins, acids and impurities and the rebuilding of the different body systems.

Personal and spiritual growth has a very definite physical component—toxins and other impurities in the body are actually part of the mechanism by which we physically structure and freeze untruthful belief patterns in the body and nervous system and thereby keep them from conscious awareness. When the brain is exposed to the brain wave patterns of deep meditation, increased amounts of energy flow through the nervous system. In the East it is said that this energy flows through a system of branching nerve channels called *nadis*, comparable to the accupuncture meridians of the Chinese healing system. According to Eastern thought, these channels constitute a subtler level of the nervous system. Wherever this flow of energy meets resistance in these channels it will cause physical release and purification. Usually this release is so subtle that it is not noticable, but in more extreme cases symptoms can include colds, sore throat, stiff and aching muscles, rashes, canker sores, sore joints, headache, fever, nausea and chills. These symptoms are identical to those induced by fasting or other common holistic health and yogic purification practices.

It is also often noted in the East that the location of symptoms may correspond to the major intersections where these channels join the spine (also called *chakras*) and that these symptoms indicate processing and clearing in that part of the energy field. Sore throats, for instance, are a sign that the throat chakra, in the Eastern view a major energy bottleneck in the body, is closing down in an attempt to block the increased flow of energy—the ego's attempt to block "dark side" feelings, memories, etc., from surfacing. Nausea, caused by secretions of the small intestine, liver and pancreas backing up into the stomach is, in the Eastern view, associated with third chakra purification dealing with issues having to do with power. Many times the location of symptoms can be a clue in uncovering deeper mental or emotional issues needing to be cleared. We offer this information not as an attempt to convert anyone to an Eastern view of things, but rather because this information has often accurately depicted or described what is happening in the experience of participants in this program.

There are other types of physical catharsis. Participants sometimes experience a kind of "antsy" feeling, a feeling, of being "over-amped," of having too much energy. This is the body's response to a more powerful energy flow through the nadis. This more powerful energy flow can also cause a tenderness around the occipital bones on one or both sides of the base of the skull.

In another variation on this theme, participants occasionally experience a tightening of the muscles in the neck and/or shoulder areas. As the two hemispheres of the brain gradually come to a point of balance over the course of a particular level of the program, they alternate in augmentation. This augmentation of one hemisphere or the other often produces resistance in the nadis which is experienced as tightness in the neck and shoulders. In the initial levels of the program this more commonly occurs in the right shoulder, corresponding to resistance in the left side of the brain, although it can occur on either side. Deeper levels of processing may tap into right brain processing in which case the symptoms will occur on the left side. (The left side of the brain controls the right side of the body and visa versa.)

There are a number of ways of dealing with these symptoms (please remember that we are merely cataloging many of the potential symptoms and that you may or may not ever have any of these). A great deal of upheaval on the physical level can be prevented through the daily practice of hatha yoga, regular aerobic exercise (such as twenty minutes on a mini-trampoline or a twenty to thirty minute walk each day) and regular bodywork sessions (massage, Rolfing, Trager, Shiatsu, etc.). Purification of the diet also effectively eliminates much physical catharsis. Other effective methods for dealing with such symptoms include alternate nostril breathing and a movement technique called the *cross crawl*, both of which bring about a balancing of the brain and a more balanced flow of energy. (See **Appendix I**)

What we are really talking about is the development of an "evolution-ary lifestyle"—doing those things on a daily basis that facilitate the natural evolutionary process, allowing the system to come to peak experience and spontaneously reorganize itself at the next higher level of awareness. Spending a few minutes each day doing some simple breathing exercises, some light aerobic exercise, and some simple yoga postures, seeing a bodyworker every few weeks, and eating a diet supportive of evolutionary change will dramatically change your experience of this program and make the whole process much easier and more enjoyable.

Another affect of meditating with Holosync is the release of endorphins, the brain's natural painkillers. This is the response of the brain to increased input as the system moves toward peak experience and reorganization at a more complex level. Endorphins are a large group of neurochemicals and each is experienced in a slightly different way. You may experience everything from light intoxication to euphoria to sleepiness. Should you begin to feel too endorphinated, the common remedy is to eat some kind of natural sugar, such as a banana or other sweet fruit (avoid refined sugars).

Some meditators experience a lot of physical catharsis, some almost none at all. Even for those who experience a fair amount of it, it comes and goes, sometimes is intense, sometimes not, and is invariably followed by increased peace and well-being. As with all types of cathartic release, the amount experienced can be controlled to a great extent by learning when to back off on the amount of meditation and by learning not to resist what is being released. Developing a relationship with a good holistic health practitioner can help you through many varieties of purificatory release.

See Appendix I for information regarding specific physical symptoms.

Emotional Release

Emotional catharsis we are all familiar with. Feelings of anger, fear, sadness, anxiety, grief and shame are common to us all. These are the emotions of a dualistic brain—a brain that divides the world into appropriate and inappropriate. As the nervous system is restructured to operate in a non-dual manner (i.e., evolves to a higher order), much emotional garbage is released.

The emotional upheaval of a meditator is very different, however, from that of a non-meditator. Meditation, especially the extremely deep meditation induced by Holosync soundtracks, very quickly develops in the meditator a kind of super-awareness—the ability to be a detached witness of what is happening. When emotional catharsis manifests as a result of meditation practice, this "witnessing" is the difference between merely venting (which may release the emotional pressure temporarily but does not shift the programming behind the emotions) and a true release and restructuring in the brain. Untruthful programming can only continue to be acted out **unconsciously** and the super-awareness induced by meditation allows this "acting out," which often occurs when unconscious programming is brought to the surface, to become increasingly conscious. To the degree that it is conscious, the energy driving the dualistic emotion falls away.

The ability to observe and deeply feel emotional catharsis without analysis or mental commentary and without unconsciously distracting oneself is one of the most important skills one can learn in this program. Anything that blocks the emotional system from coming to the point of peak experience, whether through blocking input to the system (depression or reclusiveness, for instance), distracting oneself (alcohol, drugs, sex, TV, food, etc., etc., etc.), or frantically trying to disperse the excess energy (anger, talking, exercising, compulsive behaviors, anything that disperses energy) can prevent the evolution of a new, more evolved system. It is not that these behaviors are wrong in and of themselves. However, when unconsciously used in an attempt to deal with the feeling of overwhelm that precedes the quantum leap to a new level of awareness, they get in the way of the natural evolutionary process by blocking or dispersing the very energy that, if left alone, would drive the system to evolve.

Please do not conclude that we are suggesting that emotions such as anger, fear, sadness, etc. not be felt. Evolutionarily speaking, it is absolutely necessary to feel them. It is the *unconscious acting-out* of these feelings that is many times counterproductive in an evolutionary sense because it temporarily disperses the energy that would otherwise drive the system to the next level of awareness.

Another clarification: being "conscious" of what is happening emotionally is a very subtle thing (more on this later). It is very easy to think we are being conscious when we are really dispersing energy like crazy, isolating ourself, being depressed, or distracting ourselves in some way. Just because you are "feeling" some discomfort does not mean you are being truly "conscious" of what is going on. Being conscious means feeling what is going on *fully*, without mental commentary, rationalization, or *any* resistance. It also means taking full responsibility for being the creator of your reality (this does not mean you are *to blame* for your reality, just that you know it is the projection of your unconscious programming onto "what is").

Persons who are not normally emotionally demonstrative, generally those for whom it was not safe to express themselves emotionally as children, often report that "nothing is happening" on the emotional front as they move through the first few levels of the program. In virtually all cases this is *a denial* rather than the absence of feelings. We have found that *everyone* who uses this technology, without exception, has repressed anger, fear, anxiety, etc. needing to be released. This does not mean that everyone turns into a raging maniac, it only means that these type of feelings will be surfacing, eventually, in everyone. Learning to allow yourself to experience these emotions is a necessary part of this program, and need not be overly painful.

Issues which are denied and not dealt with in the early stages of the program will reappear in each successively deeper level, but each time in a more primal and intense manner. For this reason, release is accomplished much less painfully in the early stages of the program. Often, however, the ability to see your denial and move beyond it does not develop until you have been in the program a while. If you begin with a strong commitment to self-honesty and a realization both that *everyone* has some of this emotional garbage to deal with and that there is nothing shameful about having it, you will move through whatever needs to be released with a minimum of amount of upheaval. There is no way to fake your way through this program—if you meditate with Holosync, whatever is unbalanced in you will surface to be healed and released. By trying to pretend that it isn't there, you will only make things more difficult for yourself.

Emotional catharsis manifests in many ways. Fear of the unknown may be temporarily magnified. Strong emotions—sadness, grief, anger and anxiety may arise and demand release, as may forgotten and painful memories. Conversely, you may feel euphoria, gratitude or intense joyfulness. Often these emotions seem to be unrelated or out of proportion to what is happening in the moment.

Relationships may undergo change, either becoming healthier or concluding. You may feel you no longer resonate with your old circle of friends and that new friends, more compatible with your current level of evolution, are coming into your life. These changes can be painful or not, depending on the degree to which they are resisted. As with all the changes brought about by this program, they are seen in retrospect as being highly positive.

As with physical catharsis, the amount of emotional catharsis varies from individual to individual, depending on the underlying beliefs of that individual and the amount of unresolved material needing release. Some who use this technology have a lot of emotional upheaval, some very little. As one moves through each deeper level of the program, whatever is below the surface will eventually be brought to conscious awareness. Thankfully, it is revealed with the heightened awareness necessary for its healing and release.

Should you find yourself at your peak level of tolerance emotionally, you may want to temporarily cut back on your meditation or stop entirely for a day or two (another alternative would be to go back to a previously integrated level of the program). When you feel more integrated, go back again to your regular meditation schedule. With a little experience, especially if you keep a daily journal as described in the program instructions accompanying your soundtracks, you will begin to know when you are coming to your peak level of tolerance and will be able to back off on your meditation before you become overwhelmed by your catharsis (unless your choice is to just go for it!).

If you can be in total acceptance of whatever is coming up for you, you will not be overwhelmed and there will be no need to cut back on your meditation. If you can dispassionately watch what is happening and be with whatever feelings accompany it, you will allow the dissipative structure of your brain to naturally come to the point where it will have no choice but to "escape into a higher order." This type of detached, non-judgemental witnessing typically takes several levels of the program to develop but can be developed more rapidly. It is definitely something to shoot for even in the earliest stages of the program.

**Dealing with specific emotional symptoms—
see Appendix II**

Mental Release

The last (and most prevalent) form of release we will look at is mental catharsis. In mental catharsis your mind may become busy and flooded with trivia, "old movies," or fantasies. It is possible to experience isolated, brief moments of short-term memory loss. Obsessions with food, money, sex, drugs, power and control may surface. You may feel like acting out old strategies you know to be self-destructive, but to which you still feel drawn.

But the most common and most subtle manifestation of cathartic release, mental or otherwise, is negation—negation of self, negation of others, negation of "the way things are." Physical and emotional upheaval are generally easy to spot and difficult to ignore. The same can be said for obsessive thoughts, mental busyness, fantasies and the like. Negation, on the other hand, is often very subtle, difficult to perceive, and easy to deny. Your negative, evaluating, judging voice may demand that you throw certain people or things out of your life. Other people may often appear wrong, imperfect, or inappropriate.

Negation, since is takes a certain portion of the one energy that makes up all and everything and labels it as inappropriate, is dualistic, separation-based thinking in its most crystallized form. Negation can be mind-boggling in its subtlety and always *seems* to be a justifiable response. There always seems to be a good reason for negating someone or something. As people "print out" the programming in their bio-computer as their life, there is always some reflection of their "dark side," in the world or in themselves, that they can and will negate.

A life without negation requires a total *experiential* acceptance of the perfection and interconnectedness of all things. Just being aware that one is being negative requires incredible clarity. One useful exercise which develops much awareness in this area is the keeping of a written tally of your positive versus negative responses, both to yourself and to your world, as you move through your day. This may seem like a trivial activity, yet program participants who have taken the trouble to do it report incredible shifts in awareness. Realization that negation (no matter how justifiable it seems to be in the moment) is duality (separation) thinking and a major roadblock to personal growth is a major breakthrough.

Occasionally participants uncover unconscious material they find difficult to shift or release. Working with a competent therapist will often break the logjam and get things moving again. You can also receive assistance by calling us on our Telephone Hotline at (503) 672-7117 weekdays, from 9:30 AM to 5 PM, or emailing us at support@centerpointe.com.

However, the real solution to dealing with difficult-to-shift unconscious material is to let whatever happens be okay. Keep going and trust the process. Holosync will eventually break through everything in its path, and the only way your experience can be uncomfortable is if you are resisting, either consciously or unconsciously. As you move through the program, your ability to let go will increase dramatically.

See Appendix III for for information dealing with
specific mental symptoms.

Resistance

Cathartic release is not, in and of itself, painful. *It is resistance to catharsis that causes pain.* (Resistance is duality in a nutshell—after all, what is there to resist once you realize it's all one big connected system?) Therefore, to the degree that you resist the upheaval caused by the meditation process, you will suffer. If the "dark side", as it surfaces, is embraced as but another aspect of perfection, it is easily released (or, more properly, the dualistic idea that it is inappropriate is released). Release still happens but, without resistance, the pain does not.

Unfortunately, resistance is part and parcel of the commonly held belief that the emerging "dark side" material is inappropriate. For this reason, resistance is, at least initially, unavoidable. It is only after much of the subconscious has been "cleaned out" that resistance begins to wane. There comes a point in this process, after enough healing has happened, when even the "dark side" is experienced as the perfection that is really is. What once was seen as "good" or "bad," "appropriate" or "inappropriate," now is seen as simply "happening," another part of the perfection and interconnectedness of all things. Ironically, once everything is seen as "just happening," life does not become boring or uneventful, but rather becomes peaceful, blissful, joyful.

See Appendix II for specific information concerning resistance.

The Six Stages of Evolutionary Change

~~~❧~~~

The process of evolutionary change and "escape into a higher order" as it applies to emotional and mental upheaval can be seen as occuring in six stages:

1) **Awareness**, where one first begins to realize that something is surfacing and preparing to be released, although denial is certainly still possible at this point. As this previously unconscious material comes into conscious awarensss, one may begin to experience discomfort, unrest, confusion, etc. It is in this initial stage that one begins to overcome the unconsciouness that allows untruthful belief systems to be acted out as life experience. This is the stage where different parts of the dissipative structure, due to the increased fluctuations, begin to come into contact with each other, creating new evolutionary possibilities.

2) **Identification**, where the physical sensation, feeling, thought or emotion becomes strong enough that it can no longer be suppressed, repressed or denied. At this point what is coming up can be more specifically identified ("I am feeling angry," or "I feel resistant to this.") It is important at this point not to get stuck in denial. It is a very healthy sign to be able to say "this is *catharsis*. It is not something that is happening to *me* from outside of myself, but rather a response

coming from within." (It will often *look* like it's coming from outside.) This self-honesty prepares one to take the next step:

3) **Focusing**, where the energy of the feeling, thought or emotion is heightened and *fully felt*. This is a crucial point in the process. It involves total ownership and responsibility ("This is *my* anger. I am not a victim of some outside force. I am having this feeling, this response, due to *my* particular internal programming.")

Unlike the first two stages, **focusing** requires conscious intention in order to overcome the tendency to become unconscious again through distractions such as food, drugs, sex, television, mental analysis, etc. (We tend to be more aware of the particularly destructive means of blocking out what is happening, such as drinking and drug use, but notice that there are many other ways of going unconscious that are for the most part socially acceptable. This does not mean that they are any healthier for us in a transformational sense.) By going unconscious we avoid really feeling and experiencing what is trying to happen, and block our evolution from happening.

At this point in the process we suggest using a simple technique developed by Eugene T. Gendlin, Ph.D. (which, appropriately enough, he calls "focusing") whereby one taps into subconscious material by being totally in the *felt sense* of what is going on, without mental analysis or commentary, until one experiences a *"felt shift,"* a sign, in the words of psychologist Norman Don, of "reorganization at a higher level of integration." (Those using Holosync soundtracks are particularly effective in using this technique because they spontaneously exhibit the increased alpha and theta brain wave activity which occurs immediately prior to the experience of the "felt shift".) A full description of the focusing process is beyond the scope of this booklet. We have provided a simplified form in Appendix II, but for a full explanation of this remarkable tool we encourage you to read Dr. Gendlin's book *Focusing* (1981, Bantam Books).

4) **Expansion**, where one determines the core belief system behind what is happening. In this stage one is able to generalize to past experiences and possible future situations, seeing patterns in how one's world is created. *The brain/mind computer will create whatever is necessary to prove the "truth" of its programming.* To determine what the core beliefs really are, then, it is only necessary to look at what is being created in one's world. If the creation is, for instance, unhappy relationships, the core belief may be some version of "No one will ever love me," "I am unlovable," "I have to give up my autonomy in order to be loved," etc. Another clue to core beliefs is the self-talk one experiences when in the depths of dispair ("No matter what I do, it's never good enough," "There is something wrong with me," "No one will ever love me," etc.).

This is a very crucial step in the release process. It once again involves taking ownership for what is being created. "Ownership" in this context does not imply blame (which is a form of dualistic thinking where some things are "good" and others are "bad") but simply that this is what the mind is creating, based on its subconscious programming, that this is not caused by something outside of us (though something outside may act as a trigger)—in other words, that we are not victims. By not being distracted and diverted by denial or victim consciousness (not to mention all of the other ways to distract oneself already discussed) we can honestly look at what is happening in our world and easily see what is the operative core belief behind it. At this point what was unconscious truly begins to become conscious, preparing one for the next step:

5) **Resolution**, where the energy of the feeling, thought or emotion is

experienced at its peak and fully felt, but this time in a fully conscious way. This constitutes a major shift in awareness and a totally new way for the system to disperse the necessary entropy. It is a sign that the system has come to a point of chaos (the old way of seeing and experiencing has broken down) and now has the capability to reorganize itself at a higher level.

This, more than any other step, requires conscious intention and heightened awareness. At this stage of the process you must simply *be a witness* to what is going on. This means instead of resisting the creation of the recently uncovered untruthful programming, you must watch its continued manifestation *with full awareness*. It is as if you were an intensely curious scientist, not wanting to miss a single detail of how this particular bit of programming manifests as life experience.

If the resolution is in the area of relationships, for instance, you would enter into all relationship situations curiously and carefully watching so as not to miss a single nuance of how "no one will ever love me" (if that is the operative program) is being created. If you can keep from distracting yourself and going unconscious (a big "if") you will find that it is *not possible* to continue manifesting that particular programming. The energy that had driven the program in the past simply dissipates. In the above relationship example, for instance, you would simply lose interest in continuing in the old self-destructive manner and would make other choices. It is important to note that this is *not* acomplished by trying to stop doing things in the old way, but by watching whatever is created with undivided awareness and curiousity. This awareness causes us to see the unvarnished truth concerning all the pain this particular core belief has caused us (before this point, we have remained unconscious enough to blame things on someone else, distract ourself from really feeling the pain involved, etc.) and the brain immediately seeks a new way of being that avoids this pain, i.e., it evolves. As long as we see the cause as being outside of us or distract ourself in some other way, the brain will hang onto the old way of seeing things.

Remember: simply because you are experiencing discomfort and are aware that you are experiencing your "relationship stuff" (or whatever) does not mean you are being "concious" in the sense we are using the term here. Being conscious means total ownership, total acceptance, and total awareness of the whole situation. We realize that this approach goes against how we feel like responding in these situations (especially the part about "total acceptance"), but it works!

It is in this step, therefore, that one must be particularly vigilant about remaining conscious. This means not only remaining constantly aware and in the witnessing mode while watching the creation of the recently discovered core belief, but also maintaining the awareness that what is happening is merely the manifestation of subconscious programming (not etched-in-stone "reality"); that whatever the appearance, our true nature is perfection; and that our "dark side," however unpleasant it might seem, looks "dark" only because we are seeing it dualistically through the filter of generalizations made in childhood.

Unconsciousness is an automatic response to the pain we create when we see some aspect of ourself or our world as being inappropriate. The ways in which we are tempted to go unconscious are infinitely subtle. A great deal of self-honesty and conscious awareness are required in order to recognize these distractions for what they are. Sex, drugs, alcohol, television, music, food, sports, negation, anger, dissociation, talking, reading, mental analysis, sleep, sickness, injury, illness—the list is long, the variations and subtle shadings almost endless. Our attempts to go unconscious always seem to be such justifiable, "normal," and *necessary* responses to something "out there." In actual fact, there is, of course, nothing "out there," and any manner of going unconscious only serves to block our evolution and cause us further suffering.

Because remaining fully conscious takes so much experience and practice, and because going unconscious is so easy, these core belief systems are usually not fully rescripted all at once, but rather one piece at a time. Each time another layer is peeled away it becomes easier to remain conscious the next time, until final rescripting is possible.

6) **Reintegration and reprogramming**, where the energy that was surfacing as cathartic upheaval is reincorporated into one's being. What before was a source of pain becomes a strength. No longer seen as part of the "dark side," to be repressed and avoided at all costs, and no longer a source of suffering, it now can take its place in one's consciousness as part of the flow of what is happening, part of the perfection of the infinite interrelationships that make up the universe. Out of the chaos of catharsis a new way of seeing and experiencing has evolved, one that can handle the fluctuations of "what is" without having to repress them into the unconscious, act them out as self-defeating and dysfunctional behaviors, or manifest them as various physical and health-related problems. One's brain has "escaped into a higher order," one that embraces more of the connectedness, the totality, of the universe.

The key blocks to moving through cathartic release and allowing the brain to evolve are denial and resistance. Denial is generally based in our shame (the feeling that there is somehow something wrong with us). If our family history has made expression of certain aspects of ourself not okay, the surfacing of these aspects will initially be met with denial. A backup defense often used is projection, where we make someone or something else responsible for how we are feeling. Obviously, both of these responses prevent us from seeing whatever is coming up with awareness and fully feeling it, two keys to its healing.

Developing the attitude that *whatever manifests is coming from within and is appropriate* is essential to the healing process. You may experience thoughts, emotions and other aspects of yourself that do not feel okay to you. It is important to continually remind yourself 1) that everyone has "dark side" aspects that have been suppressed; there is nothing wrong with you because these thoughts and feelings are inside of you, and 2) that whatever comes up is okay and that you can move through it. At these times you can help yourself stay in this awareness by practicing a very simple breathing exercise: breath slowly and evenly; on the in-breath say to yourself "accepting" and on the out-breath say "releasing." You will find this excercise will calm you and will reinforce your intent to see your universe as "just happening." (Please don't make the mistake of dismissing this technique [or any other seemingly simple technique discussed in this booklet] as being "too simple." These suggestions really do work and those who commit themselves to trying them report remarkable results to us.)

•••

It would be impossible to list and discuss every possible experience that one could have when meditating with Holosync soundtracks, as every person's experience is unique and depends on the contents of their own mind. We hope this discussion gives you an idea of the gamut of possible experiences and a general philosophy that will allow you to deal with anything that might arise. The important points to remember are that whatever happens is okay, that detached watching is the best remedy for nearly anything that happens, and that resistance to what is happening is your greatest obstacle. Please do not hesitate to contact us with your comments, suggestions and experiences. We are here to serve you.

It is our greatest wish that your experience of The Holosync Solution will be positive and empowering and that you, too, will experience the deep peace available to those with the courage to transcend whatever keeps them from the awareness of their true nature as happiness and love.

(Note: Suggestions in this booklet are in no way intended to constitute medical or psychiatric advice. We are not licensed medical or mental health practitioners. This material is offered from our experience and is what we have seen work in the situations cited. You must assume full responsibility for the outcome of any of these practices. If you have any questions or concerns about any of them, be sure to consult a licensed medical or mental health practitioner before using them.)

Appendixes

Appendix I — Dealing with physical release

A. **Colds, sore throat, stiff and aching muscles, rashes, canker sores, sore joints, headache, fever, nausea and chills**—these symptoms are largely the result of detoxification and can be dealt with in a variety of ways.

1) **Backing off**—if symptoms are severe, stop your use of the CDs until you feel better.

2) **Hot bath sweating**—take as hot a bath as you can tolerate; lie in the tub while the water is running in and try to stay in the bath for at least ten minutes after the tub is full. Then get out, put on a sweatshirt and sweat pants and wrap yourself in a blanket or bedspread. Lie on the floor or on a foam pad and sweat for 45 minutes to an hour. This is more effective than a sauna because you can sweat safely for much longer. When finished, drink plenty of fluids—distilled water, fruit or vegatable juices, or garlic/lemon drink (see below). A large dose (2000+ mg.) of vitamin C prior to the bath can increase effectiveness.

3) **Garlic/lemon drink**—put 2-3 large garlic cloves in a blender with the juice of two lemons, and a little fruit juice concentrate or honey to sweeten and about a pint of water. Blend together and drink.

Tastes like spicy lemonade (and much better than you would think). The garlic is a powerful blood cleanser and natural antibiotic, the lemon is a kidney flush. Taken before bed, this drink can clear up a lot of things overnight.

3) **Colonics, enemas and general colon cleansing**—in extreme cases, where much detoxification needs to be done (such as with former alcoholics, drug users or those exposed to toxic chemicals) or where a particularly toxic diet has been eaten for many years, colonics and enemas are useful. Without them, detoxification symptoms can be very intense.

For anyone, whether heavily toxic or not, colon cleansing is an extremely effective means of purifying the body and clearing lower chakra issues (those involving security, sexuality and power). This can be very effectively done on your own using herbs and other methods. A good guide to colon cleansing is *The Colon Health Handbook* by Robert Gray (Rockridge Publishing Co., 1980), available in most health food stores. Colonics alone will not effect a total colon cleansing but can be a helpful adjunct to the method outlined in *The Colon Health Handbook* or as an emergency measure during extreme physical release.

4) **Diet**—Detoxification makes little sense if you continue to put toxins into the body. We suggest the diet outlined in *Fit for Life* by Harvey and Marilyn Diamond as one way of attaining and maintaining purification on the physical level.

5) **Massage and other types of bodywork** can also be very effective in helping the body to more easily release toxins.

6) **Yoga postures**—a short 20-30 minute routine done once or twice per day can help flush the body of impurities. There are many good books on yoga for beginners and in most cities one can find of variety of yoga classes. As an instructional text, we

recommend *The Concise Light on Yoga*, by B.K.S. Iyengar (Schocken Books, 1982).

7) **Herbs** can be very useful in the detoxification process, both in purification and in the strengthening and healing of different body systems. A complete discussion of specific herbal remedies is beyond the scope of this booklet. We recommend you consult *The Way of Herbs*, by Michael Tierra, (Pocket books 1990). This book, in addition to giving much background information about herbology, gives instructions for the preparation of herbal teas and tinctures. While these are often more effective, we find that taking herbs in capsule form is also very effective and much easier. For this purpose we recommend Natures Way herbs, which can be found in most health food stores.

8) **Acupuncture and acupressure** can be very effective in treating purificatory release. Many pressure points that can be self-stimulated are discussed in the book *Own Your Own Body* by Stan Malstrom, which can be found in many health food stores. This book also contains much valuable information concerning herbs and physical purification in general.

9) **Drink purified or distilled water only**. Chlorinated tap water contains many different toxic substances and should be avoided.

10) **Develop a non-resistant attitude!** Whatever happens is okay.

B. **Feelings of being "over-amped," "antsy," too much energy.**

1) **Yoga postures**—a short 20 to 30 minute routine done once or twice per day can do a lot to smooth out and dissipate this feeling. There are many good books on yoga for beginners and in most cities one can find of variety of yoga classes. As an instructional text, we recommend *The Concise Light on Yoga*, by B.K.S. Iyengar published

by Schocken Books,1982.

2) **Purification of the diet** will go a long way toward eliminating these symptoms. We suggest the diet outlined in *Fit for Life* by Harvey and Marilyn Diamond.

3) **Massage and other types of bodywork** can also help the body more easily release these energies.

4) **Alternate nostril breathing**—This ancient technique often has an immediate effect on the symptoms mentioned above and is very effective for general energy balancing. With the right thumb, close off the right nostril and breath in through the left nostril. Release the right nostril, close off the left nostril with the ring finger of the right hand and exhale through the right nostril. Breath in, then, through the right nostril. Release the left nostril, close off the right nostril and exhale through the left nostril. This constitutes one cycle. The breaths should be only slightly deeper than normal breathing. Continue in this manner, breathing at a normal rate, for a full ten minutes. A very powerful technique which balances the hemispheres of the brain.

5) **Cross crawl**—This movement technique is similar in effect to alternate nostril breathing and is very effective in dealing with the symptoms mentioned above. Lie on your back on the floor with your hands at your sides. While slowly and deeply breathing in through the nose, gradually lift the left leg (without bending at the knee) until it is perpendicular to the floor. At the same time, gradually lift the right (opposite) arm from its position at your side until it, too, is sticking straight up. Your arm and leg should leave the floor at the same time and remain parallel to each other as they are lifted, as if connected by a metal bar.

When both are sticking straight up in the air, smoothly continue moving the arm in the same arc until it reaches the floor next to your head while the leg smoothly continues its movement by bending at the knee and bringing the knee to your chest. Completion of this whole sequence should coincide with the completion of the in-breath.

Then, as you exhale, gradually straighten the leg until it again sticks straight up, while at the same time lifting the arm from the floor next to your head to the same straight-up position. Smoothly continue the movement by lowering both arm and leg, again moving them parallel to each other so that your arm and leg touch the ground together just as your exhalation is completed. This entire sequence should be done smoothly with no stops. Repeat with your right leg and left arm. This constitutes one cycle. Continue for 25 cycles.

This is a very powerful technique and leaves one feeling balanced, refreshed and invigorated. At first it is kind of like rubbing your stomach and patting your head at the same time (your ability to do this is a good measure of coordination between right and left hemispheres of the brain). It requires a few minutes practice to master but can smooth out a number of different types of physical release.

6) **Exercise** can often help one deal with an antsy, over-amped feeling. Jumping on a mini-trampoline is very effective. It is low-impact and can be done indoors in any weather. A good time to exercise is right after meditation.

7) If symptoms are severe, **stop your use of the CDs** until you feel better.

8) **Develop a non-resistant attitude!** Remember that whatever happens is okay and is part of the process of your evolution.

C. **Tightness in the neck and shoulders** (or other parts of the body) — usually caused by resistance to increased energy flow through the nadis to one brain hemisphere or the other.

1) **Yoga postures**—see above.

2) **Hot bath sweating**—see above.

3) **Enema and colonics**—see above.

4) **Herbs**—see above.

5) **Aternate nostril breathing**—see above.

6) **Cross crawl**—see above.

7) **Massage and other types of bodywork**—see above.

8) **Develop a non-resistant attitude!**

Whatever happens is okay.

D. **Tiredness or spaciness**—This is caused by an abundance of endorphins and is a common response to the extreme expansion of awareness which happens when one is exposed to Holosync. If it becomes too much for you, eat a banana or other sweet fruit (do not eat refined sugar).

Appendix II — Dealing With Emotional Release

Our approach to emotional release is rooted in the philosophical and experiential underpinnngs of The Holosync Solution: that there is but one energy in the universe, aware of itself as all and everything. In this awareness of its all-inclusiveness, this energy is secure, happy and peaceful. This experience of security, happiness and peace is your true nature. The only way you can experience anything else is by seeing things through the filter of a dualistic brain, separating yourself from the rest of the universe and thereby either craving, fearing or becoming a victim of things supposedly outside yourself. This is unconscious living in which untruthful programming in the brain denies the unity of all and everything and creates an imperfect universe where there is always something to be done, somewhere to go, something to get, something to make better, or something to prevent in order to be happy.

Since duality is characterized by tension between polar opposites, it is both stressful and painful. The illusion of duality can be maintained only by creating a "dark side" and resisting its presence. When portions of this "dark side" come into conscious awareness, our resistance to it causes us pain. Seeing this repressed material as the perfection that it really is (instead of dualistically splitting it off from the whole and then fearing and resisting it) eliminates the pain. This usually involves "being with" the pain until the required shift in awareness happens.

This, then, is our method of dealing with emotional upheaval:

(note: see **Six Stages of Evolutionary Change** earlier in this booklet for more background on this subject.)

1) Be very clear that **whatever is happening for you is the creation of the programming in the subconscious and unconscious areas of your mind**. The connection may or may not be clear; with some situations it is obvious that you have created what is happening out of your programming, with others the connection may not be so easy to see. Regardless, know that **you are the creator**, that the universe you inhabit is created by what is in the data banks of your brain. Do not confuse this with blaming yourself for whatever is happening. Whatever happens is entirely neutral until you project your beliefs about what is appropriate and what is inappropriate onto it. Blaming yourself or others for what is happening will short-circuit the clearing process.

2) **Identify the core belief system(s) that are behind what is being**

created. This is easier than it seems, and simply involves watching what is happening. If the creation involves not getting enough love the underlying program is probably very simply "I can't get enough love," or "No one will ever love me," or "I'm not lovable." If what is happening has to do with not having enough money, the program is some variation of "I can never get my needs met," or "No matter what I do, I don't get enough." If you keep trying to please others, but seem never to succeed, the program is probably a variation of "whatever I do, it's not good enough." An inablility to have lasting relationships indicates a sub-conscious belief that you cannot have lasting relationships—it's that simple! Whatever the circumstance, the program behind it is usually very clear if you will only look, with honesty, at what is happening. (Another clue to untruthful core beliefs is the self-talk we use when in the depths of despair over what has happened: "I'll never have someone to love," "There's something wrong with me," "I can't do anything right," etc.)

To identify these core beliefs, you will also have to move beyond whatever shame you may feel about having them (shame is the feeling that there is something wrong with you). Failing to do this, you will most likely remain in denial and will be unable to shift this material and be free of it. Realize that these core beliefs are **not who you are**. You are not the body/mind mechanism or its programming, but rather the underlying energy behind it.

3) **Watching your creation**—Once you have identified the core belief behind what is happening, watch its continued creation with all the awareness you can summon. Rather than resisting its creation, or trying not to act out your typical behavior, **just watch**. The operative rule is: **non-resourceful, limiting behavior can only be created unconsciously**. If you can consciously watch what is being created

you will find that the energy behind the programming is automatically withdrawn and that things begin to unfold in new and different ways. We realize this sounds too simple to be true, but it is! (The trick is to remain conscious, which implies total ownership and total awareness of what you are creating, and a total lack of resistance.)

If you find yourself, for instance, always creating rejection in relationships, begin to enter all relationship situations *intently watching* in order to see exactly how this manifests. (This is not "expecting the worst," it is merely knowing how your subconscious operates and, with great curiousity, *watching* to see what and how it happens.) To the degree you are able to maintain *constant awareness* that you are acting out your subconscious belief concerning rejection in relationships, you will dissipate this energy and find it impossible to complete the creation. In the relationship example, you may find yourself losing interest in the type of person you usually are attracted to, or you may find the behaviors you formerly used (unconciously) to drive potential partners away are no longer happening. And, you will probably find yourself attracting a new type of person more compatible with your new level of awareness.

4) **Remaining conscious; the focusing technique**—Remaining conscious means totally "being with" (in a spirit of acceptance) whatever is happening, while at the same time being aware, moment by moment, of the programming that is behind it. This is not easy, especially in the early stages of the program. We each have an almost unlimited repertoire of strategies for going unconscious (and therefore not being with and totally feeling what is happening). Success in carrying out this step of the process is based in large part on the ability to notice when and how we do this.

One difficulty is that most of the ways we use to go unconscious seem so normal and justifiable: simple things like having something to eat, talking to friends, cleaning the house, busying oneself with a project of some kind, and exercising, just to name a few common examples, can all be ways of not being with and really feeling what is happening. Instead of falling into these distractions when something is trying to happen on the emotional front (such as anger, fear, anxiety, etc.), we recommend using a technique called *focusing* developed by Eugene T. Gendlin, Ph.D. (See Dr. Gendlin's book *Focusing*, Bantam Books,1981).

Dr. Gendlin, a professor at the University of Chicago, set out to determine what forms of therapy were the most effective. After an extensive study, he determined that no particular form was better than another; in all theraputic approaches, some patients got better and some didn't. His curiosity then led him to ask if there was something that the patients who got better had in common that helped them to move through their therapy more successfully. He found that they were naturally and unconsciously performing an internal process which he then organized into a step by step procedure and called "focusing."

The essence of the focusing technique is becoming quiet and being with the body's *felt sense* of what is happening. This means disregarding thinking, mental analysis and explanations that flash through the mind and just being with the physical feeling of what is going on. Where in the body is it located? (It may move around.) What quality does it have? Heavy? Sticky? Scary? Helpless? Oppressive? (The quality may change.) When you notice the mind offering its commentary on what is happening, where it came from, or what to do about it, tell yourself "I'll think about this later. Now I'm just feeling." Approach the feeling in your body with an intense curiosity, as if you were a scientist on the verge of a great and exciting discovery. If you can just be with what is going on, curiously watching and feeling, at some point (it may take ten minutes or it may take an hour) you will experience what Gendlin calls a *felt shift*. This is the quantum leap of the brain as a dissipative structure reorganizing itself at a new level—the sudden development of a new way of seeing things which allows a little bit of the "dark side" to now move to the "appropriate" side of the ledger. This shift can be dramatic or mundane, but it always *feels good*. (A felt shift is accompanied by endorphin release in the brain.)

You will also find even before a shift takes place that focusing on the felt sense of your anger, fear, sadness, etc. gives what is being "felt" a different quality, rendering it less painful somehow but without diminishing its intensity. This is because in approaching the feeling with curiosity the *resistance* is greatly diminished and it is the resistance to the feeling that actually causes it to be painful.

There may be times when you are in emotional upheaval but cannot take time out to do the focusing technique. While it is most effective when done in the moment, it can be done later. Very often the emotional content of an incident or situation can be evoked later by asking oneself at a later time "What is the felt sense of (describe the situation)" and then continuing with the technique. And, with some practice, it is eventually possible to learn to be with the felt sense of what is happening while in the midst of doing other things. (A full explanation of the focusing technique is beyond the scope of this booklet. We urge you to read Dr. Gendlin's book for yourself.)

5) **Breathing and awareness**—Another way we go unconscious and block our felt experience is through shutting down our breathing. You may notice that when you are in emotional upheaval you often forget to breath. This can prevent feelings from surfacing. It also diminishes any potential for evolutionary shifting of awareness by limiting the

amount of energy entering the system. Remind yourself in these situations to breathe; take slow deep breaths and allow yourself to feel what is happening. You may even want to try some more sophisticated breath work such as Holotropic breathing, developed by Christina and Stan Grof. Holotropic breathing is a very powerful method of accessing and clearing subconscious patterns, and can be an excellent adjunct to The Holosync Solution (for more information concerning Holotropic breathing therapy visit www.holotropic.com).

6) **Backing off** —Should you reach your peak level of tolerance emotionally you may want to back off on your use of Holosync until you feel more integrated.

7) **Therapy and the Telephone Hotline**—If you have tried all of the suggestions offered in this booklet and still are having trouble dealing with what is coming up for you, you may want to talk to a therapist. It is not necessary that your therapist be familiar with this technology. (We would be happy to discuss your situation with your therapist if you like.) Also, please remember that we are available to speak with you on the telephone from 9:30 AM to 5 PM, Pacific Time, Monday through Friday. The Hotline number is (503) 672-7117. You may also email your questions or concerns to us at support@centerpointe. com. We have many years of experience in dealing with every kind of occurance and often a short conversation can help shift something that has been bothering you for weeks, months, or even years. Those who consistently use the Telephone Hotline seem to progress much faster and have a much easier time processing the changes that are taking place for them. Use the Hotline!

8) **Don't resist!**—One other prescription for dealing with emotional release bears repeating: develop a non-resistant attitude! We have seen again and again in our work with persons moving through very intense

release that *it is not what is coming up that is painful, it is your resistance to it.* Get in the habit of reminding yourself that the resistance you feel is created by untruthful duality-based thinking and that there is really nothing that can harm you, nothing that you cannot successfully move through. Use the "accepting—releasing" breathing technique described earlier or any other method that reminds you that everything is unfolding just as it should.

Internal Representations

It is very interesting to note that we store our internal representations of those things we resist and those things we accept in different ways, each sending certain specific neural signals to the brain, thereby creating certain specific mental and emotional states. These internal representations have three major modalities: 1) visual, 2) auditory, and 3) kinesthetic (feeling). In other words, we create internal representations of the outside world in some combination of internal pictures, sounds, and feelings, and the different ways in which we do this creates our different experiences of the world.

In representing an event that we find appropriate, we might, for example, place the picture in a specific location and make it a certain size with a certain amount of brightness focus. An event we find inappropriate might be placed in a different location, with a different size and a different amount of brightness and focus. Auditorily, the sounds might be of different volumes and originate from different locations. And, the feelings in the body might be very different, as well. For most people, these internal representations flash by instantaneously, out of our conscious awareness. Nonetheless, they are the brain's way of making distinctions—it is by this mechanism that we discriminate between good or bad, past and future, believed andnot believed. We can use this information to quickly shift to more resourceful beliefs .

Incredibly, when we take an experience that we find inappropriate, (and therefore are negating and resisting) and change these internal components (location, size, brightness, focus, etc.) from those that we use for storing inappropriate experiences to those that we use for appropriate experiences, our outlook and experience of that event *automatically shifts* because we are now sending signals to the brain to view this particular event as appropriate.

The implication here is that nothing is intrinsically appropriate or inappropriate, but that by our *internal representation of that event* we experience it as one or the other. In this way, we create our own individual experience of reality.

Spend a few minutes internally recreating an event or situation that you experience as appropriate. Let an internal picture come to you. Note its location in your visual field, its size, its brightness, and its degree of focus. Then do the same for an event or situation that you experience as inappropriate. By moving the "inappropriate" picture to the location of the "appropriate" picture, and making it the same size, brightness and focus, you will send messages to your brain that this experience is actually appropriate and will create a new and more empowering experience. Since we know that resistance to "what is" slows our evolution, this is an extremely valuable tool that can create results quickly and save you much pain by moving you out of resistance easily and effortlessly.

Appendix III — Dealing with mental release

A. **Busy mind, fantasies, obsessions, trivia, "old movies,"**

etc.—Realize that this is just the "running off" of the material in the subconscious mind. This material has no power to do anything and should be dispassionately observed. Either resisting what comes up or clinging to it will short-circuit the evolutionary process. The Buddhists have a saying: "If you meet the Buddha in your meditation, kill him immediately." In other words, no matter what the mental activity, no matter how compelling, do not get caught up in it, even if it is a heavenly vision of God. Just watch. Treat all mental phenomena as clouds in the sky, just drifting by. To just be a witness to your mental catharsis is the most powerful advice we can give.

B. **Negation**—Dealing with negation involves 1) the awareness that it is happening in the first place, 2) the knowledge that negation is dualistic and dis-empowering thinking, regardless of how justifiable it may seem in the moment, 3) being the silent witness, and 4) working with internal representations (see Appendix II). Much of what was suggested regarding dealing with emotional release applies to mental release as well, especially the focusing technique, non-resistance, the use of therapy, and the suggestion to back off on your use of the CDs if you reach your peak level of tolerance. Also see **Six Stages of Evolutionary Change** earlier in this booklet.

C. **Depression**—You may from time to time experience minor depression as you move through the various levels of the program. Depression is a form of resistance to powerful data trying to emerge into conscious awareness, and is characterized by a repression or shutting down of one's energy in an attempt to not experience this emerging data. The dissipative structure of the brain, desperately trying to keep the existing system stable as it comes to the point of peak experience, generally tries to uplevel its attempts to dissipate the amount of entropy necessary to keep the system viable. In the case of depression, however, the attempt is to block incoming fluctuations from the environment as a way of reducing the amount of entropy needing to be dissipated. Oxygen consumption is lowered, adrenal gland and other metabolic function is curtailed, appetite often falls off and even the pupils of the eyes contract in order to take in less light.

Therapists familiar with an approach called Neuro Linguistic Programming (NLP) have noticed that feeling "down" is often accompanied by a downcast look—an actual looking downward (we tend to unconsciously look in different directions as a way of accessing different parts of the brain), as well as a feeling of wanting to lie down. Quite dramatic shifts in depression can often be accomplished by increasing oxygen intake through deep, connected breathing and by exercise and other movement approaches such as Bio-Energetics, Feldenkreis, etc which serve to "charge" the body energetically (see the book Bio-Energetics by Alexander Lowen); and by changing the physical orientation to one of standing up and looking up instead of lying down and looking down—in general, by changing the modality from de-energized to energized and from "down" to "up." While these may seem like minor changes, they have a powerful effect on the brain and on depression.

Once the depression is shifted, powerful feelings, previously masked by the deprssed state, may arise. Remember to use the focusing technique at this point. Be with and watch what is happening with a minimum of mental analysis and commentary. (See the book *Focusing* by Eugene Gendlin, Bantam Books, 1981.)

Severe clinical depression can be very serious. We are speaking here of intermittent, acute depression associated with cathartic release. If you are having severe or long-lasting depression, see a doctor or therapist.

Remember also to use the Telephone Hotline (503-672-7117) if you need help, or have any questions or comments. We are here to serve you weekdays from 9:30 AM to 5 PM, Pacific Time.

Suggested Reading

1. Gendlin, Eugene T., Ph.D., *Focusing* (Bantam Books, 1981.)

2. Gray, Robert, *The Colon Health Handbook* (Rockridge Publishing Co., 1980.)

3. Iyengar, B.K.S., *The Concise Light on Yoga* (Schoken Books, 1980.)

4. Lowen, Alexander, *Bio-Energetics*, (Penguin Books, 1980.)

5. Tierra, Michael, *The Way of Herbs*, (Pocket Books, 1990.)